Google Classroom

Classroom

The Top 5 Hidden Features To Master Google Classroom For Teachers And Students. Boost The Quality Of Online Teaching And Improve Your Students' Engagement

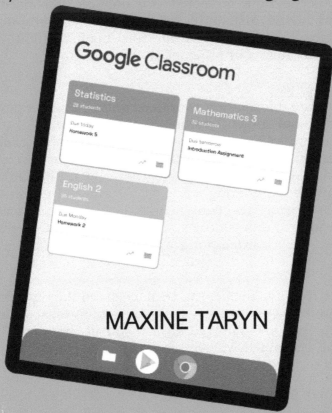

MAXINE TARYN

E-LEARNING

Table of Contents

Introduction

Benefits of Google Classroom

What Google Classroom aims to form the event, distribution, and grading of assignments easy and during a way that doesn't involve the use of paper. Overall, the underlying objective of Google Classroom is to make a direct link that files are often shared between students and their teachers.

Next, we'll discuss the benefits of using Google Classroom:

Simple-to-Use Tool

Google Classroom offers an exceptionally intuitive and excessively simple-to-learn interface. The platform talks you through each progression of the procedure. It's anything but difficult to utilize. "Google Classroom's build-up makes the educational interface simple, and options used for conveying for following-up assignments correspondence with the entire course or people is additionally rearranged through announcements, e-mail, and message pop-ups. At the purpose, once you land on the most page of your classroom, you will be welcome to "communicate together with your class here." You'll establish announcements and program them to travel out on your own time. You'll also answer student notes. The interface is straightforward to understand, which means that there is no individual learning or adaptation required to utilize the software. Google classroom is anything but complicated.

Class Creation and Student Addition

Google Classroom allows you to make a class for every class you instruct. You'll create a category and the Classrooms are partitioned into various areas.

In the Students' area, you'll see all the participants currently in your class. Students are often added manually, or they will join on their own utilizing their own Google account. At the purpose, once you create a category from their PCs or Chromebooks, students sign into their Google files and utilize that to code to hitch.

Inside the scholar segment, you'll likewise decide whether your students are permitted to remark on the questions, announcements, and assignments you create or if they will just post in the least. If you would like, you'll plan to be the one most who can post and remark in your class.

In the stream area, you'll discover the assignments, announcements, and questions that you simply create. This area is where you'll invest the bulk of your energy after your classes are found out.

In the educator area, here, teachers can streamline how they oversee classes furthermore since the platform incorporates alright with other Google tools. For instance, Drive, Doc, and Calendar are bunches of inherent accessible routes or shortcuts for classroom management responsibilities. For example, when assignments are posted with due dates, they automatically are added to the category schedule for college kids to ascertain.

Using Google Classroom Assignments

Assignments are a unique method utilized in gathering student work and providing them with feedback and grades. At the purpose, once you create a task, you'll give explicit instructions to that task, a maturity, and a topic. During a case, once you incorporate a timeline for the job, students will have until 11:59 PM on the date to present their work for that assignment. When they offer the work late, Google Classroom, despite everything, indicates a turn in late when it acknowledges the task.

Perhaps the simplest element of the Google Classroom Assignments is that you simply can add files to the assignments you create. You'll include a document from your PC, a file from Google Drive, a YouTube video, or a link to an internet site. A business instruction educator can allocate writing briefly on an individual within the news, then add a link to a YouTube video of that individual giving a speech.

Students can present any kind of file in your Classroom. Not only would students be ready to give their finished work as files, but you'll also open them directly from the Classroom and grade them. Open documents submitted to your Classroom as long as your PC has an online association. Therefore, the software is expected to open the file, and you do not get to get on your school PC!

For instance, you'll assign an exposition, and your students can present that in your Google Classroom from any PC that has an online association. You'd then be ready to open the document and grade it on your PC at college or home. This medium gives you extra time during class to consider pushing ahead, rather than sitting around idly gathering work.

Communication and Collaboration

One component of Google Classroom is creating collaboration; for instance, questions, send announcements, and instant beginning class conversations. Educators can likewise rapidly observe who has or hasn't finished the work, and provides immediate, ongoing feedback and grades. Google Classroom makes it easy to watch a student work. Right from the scholar Work screen, click on any student's task thumbnail to ascertain real-time advancement.

You can find out what an issue is worth point-wise and even permit students to attach. Students can share materials and communicate within the class stream or by e-mail. A simple-to-access platform encourages interaction, even in a web environment, and allows students to realize from one another.

Google Classroom allows you to pose an issue inside a specific class. Similarly, like assignments, you'll add documents to the questions you post and may allocate a maturity. You'll post a brief answer or different decision questions for your students to reply to within the Classroom. As they answer a particular decision question, Google Classroom organizes the outcomes for that question then shows you the breakdown of the students' answers progressively. At the purpose, once you click on one among the multi-choice solutions, the Classroom shows which students picked that choice.

When students answer a brief question, Google Classroom can't classify the outcomes, showing student responses. By then, you'll remark or reply to each student, and provides evaluation as you see fit.

Notwithstanding making assignments and questions, Google Classroom permits you to make announcements. Students can then answer your decisions, and you furthermore may respond, thereby creating a string. The entire class can have a discussion hooked into one announcement. By and by, you have the choice of including a file, YouTube video, or a connection to a statement.

Announcements are a unique method to post a reminder about task due dates to your students. You'll even schedule reports to post sometime within the future, which may assist you with remaining sorted out, also like your students. Indeed, even classroom teachers can utilize the announcement feature to post reminders, consent forms for field trips, materials, just in case students lose them, and the list goes on.

In addition to the scholars cooperating, educators interacting with singular students can likewise interface with guardians/parents (although this is often confined to e-mails). The many interactive mediums may incorporate e-mail, post to a stream, private remarks, and feedback.

Engagement

Most digital locals are comfortable with innovation and can be progressively ready to take possession of their learning through change. The classroom gives various approaches to make learning intuitive and communitarian. It offers educators the capacity to separate assignments, incorporate videos and site pages into exercises, and make community-oriented gathering assignments.

It's been demonstrated multiple times that students are locked in by innovation. Google Classroom can assist students with arising to be and remain occupied with the training procedure. During a situation where you've got students answering questions within the Classroom, different students can remark on these answers and develop thought for the others.

One of the foremost vital features of Google Classroom is that it permits you to debate better together with your students outside the four walls of a classroom. Formerly, students got to be within the course for teachers to ask them an issue. But now teachers can roll in the hay whenever and anywhere.

Just in case you've got a Google Account through your region, the Classroom is just staying there standing by to help you with testing and engaging your students. Generally, utilizing Google Classroom is undoubtedly advantageous. It can spare you an excellent deal of your time and energy and may assist you to prepare your students for what's to return. The classroom gives students an introduction to an online learning system. Numerous school and college programs currently expect students to undertake out, at any rate, one online class. Exposure to Google Classroom may assist students with progressing into another learning management system utilized in advanced education.

Saves Time

Teachers can create classes, disperse assignments, communicate, and remain organized, beat one place. All everything of the scholars, data, entries, and grades are in one convenient area. For college kids, all the materials for a category are in one single space. There is no compelling reason to seek out a book, get your journal, drive to a classroom for a lecture, or print out a piece of writing. Instead, you'll see the exercise online, answer questions, and even submit work across the board area. Everything remains slick and sorted out along these lines, and time isn't squandered, checking out lost classroom materials. Google Classroom coordinates and automates other Google applications, including docs, slides, and spreadsheets. The way toward managing file distribution, grading, developmental evaluation, and feedback is simplified and streamlined. A couple of highlights like expert grade to Google Sheets, more straightforward to update mark scale, console route for entering grades, sort by name on grading page then forth., spare educators' time.

Differentiating Between Skill Levels

Google Classroom allows you to separate different skill levels by fixing an equivalent number of varied classrooms as you want. One model may act automatically guided reading projects. You'll have two or three groups of scholars utilizing the program. However, Class A could also be at a sixth-grade understanding level, Class B at a fourth-grade understanding level, and sophistication C at a second-grade understanding level.

With Google Classroom, you'll isolate each group so that they work at their own pace. You'll likewise observe all of your students from an equivalent dashboard and type out who needs extra assistance, and which students exceed expectations within the topic and wish all the more of a test.

Through the Classroom, educators are effectively able to separate instruction for college kids. Allocating exercises to the whole class, singular students, or groups of scholars takes only a few straightforward steps when making an assignment on the Classwork page.

Work Isn't Lost

Google Classroom is cloud-based, and intrinsically, they present professional and credible technology to use in learning conditions as Google applications communicate to "a significant segment of cloud-based venture communication tools utilized during the skilled workforce. All documents transferred by teachers and students are put away during a Classroom folder on Google Drive.

Work in Google Classroom saves automatically and may be accessed from any gadget. Students can work flawlessly anywhere there, without agonizing over cumbersome flash drives, messaging files to and fro, or losing progress due to PC glitch. "I left it reception," and "My PC malfunctioned before I could save," are not any longer excuses you will need to interact.

Chapter 1: Chapter 1 Google Classroom and Other Platforms

Google Classroom is a learning center that can be dedicated to any level of education and also is designed to help find answers to the challenges encountered in creating assignments without the use of paper. The use of Google Classroom may be through multiple platforms, such as via computers and devices. The many services provided by Google will make it much easier for instructors and teachers to carry out learning practices. The desired learning is not just in class, but also outside of the class, because students can learn anywhere and anytime when they access Google classroom online.

Using Google Classroom makes the learning experience more efficient, and both educators and students will face each other at any time via Google Classroom online classes. Content files posted to the Classwork bar can be Word, PowerPoint, Excel, PDF, video files, or simulation files. The material provided in this implementation also applies to the everyday lives of students. This is done by educators to accommodate distinctions in the rate of thinking, background information, and differences in student learning styles. To start using Google Class, log in to your Google Account first, and check the product. After signing in to the Google classroom account, we face three main menus: Streams, Classwork or student activities, and People.

Apple Classroom vs. Google Classroom

Apple Classroom is an educational product from Apple. Many educators believe they are the same thing from different companies. While they bear similar names and are built to bring technology to the classroom, there are several differences between both products. Here is how both products compare.

Apple Classroom

Apple Classroom was launched in March 2016, bringing Apple closer to education. Apple Classrooms is available as a free app for Apple iPads and iPhones as well as online. Apple allows the teacher to monitor students' work from an iPad or Mac computer, allowing classroom management. Students' privacy is secure, as class records are kept private. Students are notified when the teacher views or projects their screen. With Apple Classroom, a student must not own the devices they use. It works perfectly with iPads with multiple users (shared devices).

Using Apple Classroom, teachers can connect to nearby devices and assign students to shared iPads and log them out of the device after a class. Teachers can monitor and control students' work by starting or pausing student work. The teacher has substantial control over student devices and can launch webpages, apps, or documents on student devices from his device. The teacher can also lock the device on a single app, view student activity on the app, or mute audio on student devices.

One downside of Apple Classroom is that this product is limited to only Apple devices. Students will have Apple devices for it to work. Apple Classroom, however, easily syncs with Google apps and solutions. With Apple Classroom, you can easily project items from your iPad unto larger Apple TV screens and use Airplay. You can integrate games from third party sources in Apple Classroom.

Teachers can reset forgotten passwords. They also can split the class into groups to carry out projects and tasks. It can be done directly from the teacher's app before been pushed to the students.

Google Classroom

Google Classroom works across almost all devices. Teachers and students can use android and non-android devices to access Google Classroom. There is no limitation to what sort of device they can use. This ability to integrate across devices, platforms, and even apps and other similar programs make Google Classroom stands out. You have hundreds of apps and extensions you can add to make your Google Classroom experience more powerful.

Google Classroom stands out for its superb workflow management. Its integration with Google productivity apps and other third-party apps allows the teacher to connect with students in a few other solutions can. This teacher-student connection allows workflow from the teacher's Google Drive to the student's Google Drive and vice versa.

Google Classroom makes sharing information easier when is compared to other Learning Systems like Apple Classroom. On Google Classroom, you can share digital resources easily with students. Also, you can share the significant resources on the stream, which serves to streamline, house, and archive vital information.

The integration with other productivity tools from Google helps users integrate due dates from assignments into Google calendars. It allows the Calendar to be viewed across devices and when customized by other parties like parents. The ease of bringing materials from outside Google Classroom puts it miles ahead of similar software.

From the above comparisons, you will tell the significant differences between Apple Classroom and Google Classroom.

Apple Classroom provides more substantial classroom management rights to the teacher. The teacher has greater control over student devices with Apple Classroom. It is, however, limited by the fact that it can only work when the teacher and students own Apple Devices, unlike Google Classroom that is not device-dependent.

Google Classroom's ability to seamlessly integrate with Google productivity tools and third-party apps gives it a winning edge. While Google Classroom and Apple Classroom are both used in the classrooms, they have different objectives. The teacher can, however, make use of both to achieve better learning in the classroom.

New Features of Google Classroom

As Google Classroom has enjoyed more widespread use, new features and benefits have come out. These are meant to make it easier for both teachers and students to get more out of this platform and find it easier to use. Some of the most recent updates to the Classroom include:

• Quizlet Class: With this update, the teacher can create a Quizlet at the same time they create the class. Once the account is set up, you can set up the account and link both of these together. When students join the class, Quizlet will notify them at the same time.

• Upload playing tests: This one is useful for music classes. Students will be able to record playing tests or upload one they have already done. The teacher can then view the playing test and leave their feedback. Students can choose to listen to the test again to make improvements or ask questions if something doesn't make sense.

• Outside of class viewing party: Many live events can help with a particular topic, but which may be hard to take the whole class too. For example, live performances, debates, speeches, and even movies could help the teacher talk about specific points. If these live events happen after class hours, the teacher can incorporate them into the class and add live posts and discussions to keep students working together.

• Warm-up questions: If the teacher would like to assess how well students understood the class or perhaps do a quick view before a test, the warm-up question feature can help. Post the questions and let students either put in an essay answer or multiple choice. This feature doesn't allow students to see other answers, so you know how each one thinks without influence from their peers.

• Flubaroo: This is a great add-on that allows some homework assignments and tests to be graded immediately. Assignments that use multiple choice questions and true and false statements will enjoy Flubaroo because students can submit the work and receive feedback right away. It saves time for the teacher, allows students to see which questions they got wrong, and speeds up the learning process.

• Class discussions: One cool feature of the Classroom is the ability to have several classes talk together. Teachers can connect with other teachers in the same or similar classes, and students can share ideas and discussions.

• Photo assignments: Students can even watch the classroom on a smartphone and tablet and use their cameras to complete projects. Send students on a scavenger hunt, let them upload a picture of their homework, or use the camera in another way.

• Forums: Forums are another way to expand on the class discussion, making it easy for a whole grade level to converse together and share their knowledge. The school can set up several teachers and administrators to watch the comments of the whole school. Younger students can ask questions about which classes to take, for example, and older students can find out about colleges, how their credits work, and so on.

• Poll questions: All teachers can use a poll question, but it works particularly well for math teachers. They can turn a math problem into a poll to use the skills they learn in class to come up with an answer. This feature also works well for teachers to gather feedback.

• Guided reading: Test vocabulary; make students answer questions as they get through parts of a reading assignment. Help them make sure the whole class understands essential concepts before moving on.

• Post a link: Posting links can bring in outside sources for students to learn even more. The teacher can add digital resources and videos.

• Parent support: Google has added a feature that allows teachers to communicate with and keep parents updated on student progress. The parents will need to sign up for the class. Then, they will receive a weekly update and e-mail digests, so they can keep track of upcoming assignments, all important announcements, and how well their student is doing in class. It makes it easier for parents to participate in learning without taking up valuable teacher time.

• Teacher control: Teachers have full control over the classroom. They will decide when something is appropriate and may need to 00Gstep if comments don't stay on topic or students begin to attack each other. The classroom has made this easy for the teacher to control what is going on at all times.

As time goes on, Google Classroom will add more great features that make it easier for teachers and students to work together inside and outside the classroom. Teachers can already enjoy being in charge of the Classroom, posting important announcements, handing out assignments without wasting time and paper, and communicating with students. In a world where education is always changing and time is valuable, Google Classroom could answer that schools need to get the work done without all the stress and wasted time.

Chapter 2: Chapter 2 How to Use Google Classroom for Teachers

One of the first things you do as a teacher in Google Classroom is to create a class for each group of students you tutor. After you have created a class, you can begin to assign work, post announcements, and facilitate online discussions.

If your school has a G-Suite for Education account, you can use the e-mail to create a class. Also, you can use your personal Google account to create classes as long as you are above 13 years of age.

To Create a Class on Your Android/iOS Mobile Phone

1. Click on the Classroom app.

Google Classroom

Classroom helps classes communicate, save
time and stay organised. Learn more

2. Tap the ((+)) sign > Create class.

3. Input the class name.

4. Tap Pane and enter a short description, grade level, class time, and other information (optional).

5. Enter your location for the class by selecting Room (optional).

6. Add the subject by tapping the Subject and then enter the name (optional).

7. Select Create.

Once you are done creating your class, Google Classroom instantly issues a class code. It is this class code that you use to invite students to the class. You can view the class code on the Stream page.

To Create a Class on Your Computer

1. Go to Google Classroom

2. Click on the (+) sign at the top-right corner > Create class.

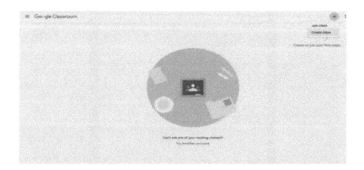

3. Input the class name.

4. Enter a short description, grade level, or class time by clicking pane. It is below the Class name field. This step is optional

5. If you want to add a subject, tap the Subject. Input the name or click one from the list of names that appears when you enter the text.

6. If you wish to enter your location, click Room and input the details.

7. Tap Create.

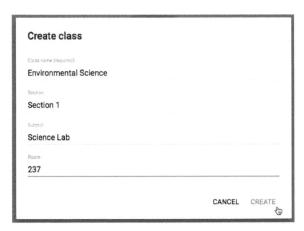

Inviting Students to Your Class

Once you are done creating your class, the next thing is to invite your students. Invite them via e-mail (manually). You can make it with the steps below:

1. Click on the class that students need to register.

2. Navigate to the People Tab.

3. Click on the Invite student's icon.

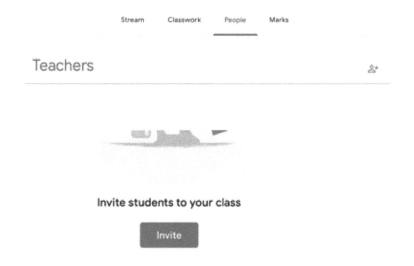

4. A search box would then be brought up to look for the e-mail address of each student.

Invite students

Invitation link

https://classroom.google.com/c/MTc1OTEwODg4MjIz?cjc=koc...

Type a name or email address

Cancel   Invite

5. Once you're done adding, click Invite. It will send an e-mail notification to your students with a link inviting them to join your online class. It is one method teachers typically skip because it is labor-intensive.

6. Inviting students via Classroom code is another way of inviting students to your class. It is an easier way to accomplish this is by having students join on their own via a class code. It is used by the students to join your class if you provide them with the code. To access it:

7. Go to Google Classroom.

8. Click on the class setting icon.

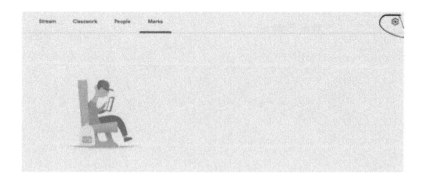

9. You will find the class code. Write it down, or better still, copy it; share the code with your students however you'd like.

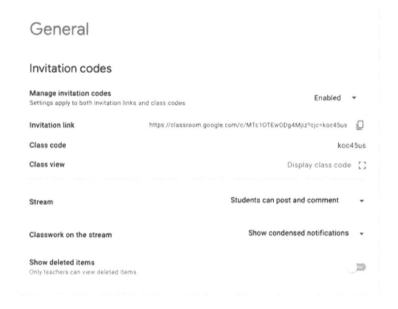

General

Invitation codes

Manage invitation codes
Settings apply to both invitation links and class codes   Enabled ▾

Invitation link   https://classroom.google.com/c/MTc1OTEwODg4Mjlz?cjc=koc45us 🔲

Class code   koc45us

Class view   Display class code ⟦⟧

Stream   Students can post and comment ▾

Classwork on the stream   Show condensed notifications ▾

Show deleted items
Only teachers can view deleted items

10. Learners can log in through the class code, which adds them to your class right away.

Note: The teacher can disable or change the class code when necessary. Just select the drop-down menu and disable/reset the code when you need to. Students who are already registered will not be affected by this action.

Inviting Teachers to Your Class

You may also include a co-teacher to help you in your activities. You can do this through Google Groups, where you can invite co-teachers to the group.

Typically, the G-Suite administrator from your school will allow students and teachers to be part of classes. If you need to include an outside person, you may need to inform your admin to update the settings.

To invite a co-teacher to your class:

1. Click on the class in which a teacher will be co-teaching with you.

2. Hover your mouse over the People button.

3. Select Invite Teachers.

4. Input your co-teacher's e-mail address. Google Classroom will automatically show addresses that match the one you are looking for.

5. From the search results, click on the particular teacher.

6. Select Invite.

7. Accepting an invitation as co-teacher in Google Classroom

8. When someone invites you as a co-teacher, you will receive an e-mail from Google. To be part of the class, just select Accept.

9. Also, there is some permission co-teacher(s) need to be aware.

10. The primary or principal teacher has the sole right to delete the class.

11. Co-teachers cannot be removed or unrolled by the primary teacher from the class.

12. Muting teachers is not allowed.

13. The class Google Drive folder is with the primary teacher.

14. After joining the class, the co-teachers also have access to the class Google Drive folder.

15. Editing, Moving or Archiving a Class.

If it is your first time on Google Classroom, test classes may be necessary to get the hang of the application, to see how it works or what it offers. In creating a test class, follow these steps:

1. Select the Menu tab. It is found at the upper-left side of the monitor.

2. Click Classes to enable you to see your created Classrooms

3. Click on the set of dots on the upper-right side of a particular Classroom where you need to make changes.

4. To effect the needed changes, select Move, Edit, or Archive

5. The Move tab is for rearranging the classes order on your dashboard. Meanwhile, the Archive tab is for removing Classrooms from the dashboard and archiving them. You can access to an archived by clicking Archived Classes in the Settings tab. You can either restore an Archived class or delete it permanently.

Altering How Your Class Looks

You are given an original layout picture right when your class is created. When students click on your group to get announcements and assignments, this is the picture they will see. This image can be customized to suit your class with a few quick steps:

1. Changing the theme.

2. Hover your mouse on the banner image.

3. At the bottom-right side, look for the Select Theme link.

4. You can open your photo gallery and select a theme for your class.

5. To change the original image that came with creating your class, select theme from your photo gallery.

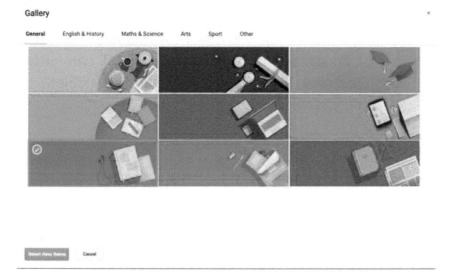

6. There, you will find an assortment of pictures to browse from. However, most themes you will find are on the academic subject. For example,

you could pick books for Language Art Classes, a piano for Music, a hued pencil for Art, etc. You can likewise transfer your photograph by tapping the Upload photograph link.

Adding a Syllabus

A teacher can create and allocate work for their students through the help of Google Classroom. Worksheets, questions, essays can be shared and made available online to your class in a paperless format.

1. Navigate to the Classwork tab.

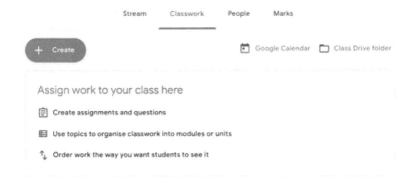

2. Click Create and then choose questions and materials. You can also view all current and past assignments.

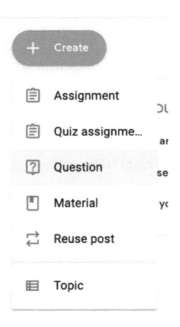

3. Add a title, description, and any other attachments you desire for your class.

4. Click Topic and then assign your materials to a new topic called Syllabus

5. Click on Post when you are done.

For

Computer Sc... ▾   All students ▾

6. Materials can be assigned to multiple classes or even to individual students if needed. You can choose the alternative you need from the upper-left corner when creating another material for your class.

7. If you want your syllabus topic to be on top of your class page, select the arrows at the upper-right corner of the topic, and select Move Up. You can repeat as often as necessary. Another way to get this done is to relocate Topics or Materials by clicking and hauling up and down on the Classwork page.

Assignment Creation in Google Classroom

You can create and send assignments to students in Google Classroom. Here are some useful options for teachers to take advantage:

1. Go to the class in which you will create a particular assignment.

2. On the topmost part of your interface, select the Classwork tab.

3. Select the Create tab, and then click the Assignment or Question if you would like to post a single question to your students.

4. Give a title to your assignment and include any additional description or instructions in the box provided for that purpose.

5. Set your deadline by clicking Date, and then add time should you need to determine when it is due.

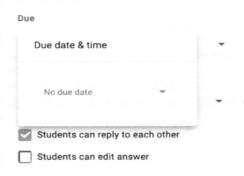

Due

Due date & time

No due date

✓ Students can reply to each other

☐ Students can edit answer

6. Select the assignment type by tapping on the symbol beside the Assign tab. You can upload or attach any file, including a video from YouTube, or share a website link.

Select assign once you have completed the form. An e-mail notification message would be sent to the class, letting know about the assignment. For future reference, you can schedule the assignment to be saved and posted later. It can be posted to multiple classrooms by clicking the class name on the Assignment window at the upper-left corner and picking the classes of your choice. All the assignments are gathered by Google Classroom and automatically added to your Calendar. On the Classwork tab, you can easily click on the calendar icon to get a better holistic view of the timeline of the due dates of all your assignments.

Also, while creating an assignment, there may be times when you need to append an archive from Google Docs. These can be useful while giving protracted directions, study modules, and other materials. When attaching these types of files, you'll make sure you chose the correct setting for how your students can interact with it. A drop-down menu will appear as soon as you're done attaching one to the assignment, with the following three options:

Students can view files: This option is to be used if the teacher wants only the students to view files and not to make any changes to it. It is perfect for study and nonexclusive gifts that the entire class needs access to.

Students can modify/edit file: This option is to be used when the document provided needs to be worked on in groups either as an in-class project or individually. Students can work on individual slides on the same presentation, or they can cooperatively conceptualize thoughts for the next topic.

Make a separate copy for every student: This option is used to create a separate duplicate of the same document for the students in the class to complete and to permit them to edit the file. The original copy that belongs to the teacher remains untouched, and access to it is restricted. This option is to be chosen if you prefer the rapid dissemination of a paper with a template. Students will just supply their answers on the blanks provided.

1. In the box for Assignments, the number of students who have turned in their assignments and the number of those who haven't will be displayed.

2. Click on the number of those who have submitted their assignments.

3. Expand any student's assignment by clicking on his name.

Chapter 3: How to Use Google Classroom for Students

This is a complete guide for any student looking to sign up for and study only with Google Classroom. We'll talk about everything from login to assignments to Stream posts. Also, we will give you in-depth, step-by-step instructions on how to create assignments and how to turn them in. Furthermore, this will also guide you on how to post a query in the Stream and how to answer questions posted by your instructor in the Stream and much more.

Student Login

- Go to Google Classroom.

- You will see the homepage display when you first turn up at the Google Classroom web site.

- Scroll to the bottom, and choose your role as a student.

Join the Classroom

- Go to the Google Classroom. If you are logging in first, be sure to pick your role as a student.

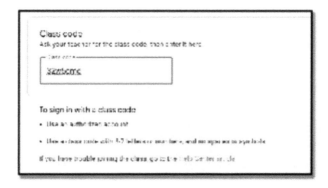

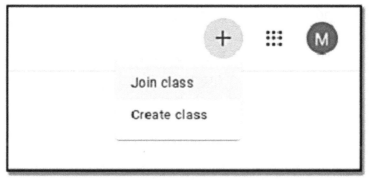

- To Join class, click the + at the top right of the page.

- Type your professor's Class code, and press "Join."

The Stream

The Stream is where learners can monitor and track updates, homework, subjects for debate, and feedback. Students may also attach posts and leave feedback if allowed by the instructor.

Add Student Post to the Stream:

- Press the + button on the monitor, and then pick Build Post.

- Add your Class Post text. Remember, your instructor and the whole class can view this.

- Use the post to raise specific questions regarding lessons or tasks, to interact with other students in your school, or to exchange the critical class subject and topic information.

Note: Your responses are stored, even after deletion. Your instructor will still see what you're saying, so keep it appropriate.

You can add other material to your posts, as an option:

- **File Attachments:** Locally saved files on your computer or smartphone.

- **Google Drive**: Saved files on your Google Drive.

- Videos on YouTube

- Links to third-party websites, materials, etc.

Assignments

Uploaded assignments are shown in the Stream. To see the latest updates, you may be urged to refresh the Stream or Assignment. Students do have the opportunity to leave a note for class if the instructor has allowed this. The educator and other learners in the class are eligible for post-class feedback. For each assignment, the learners will see the following details and options in the Stream.

- Current status (not finished or finished.

- Closing Date (learners can even see if the assignment is late).

- Description and title of the assignment.

- **Open:** press this button to open the details page for the assignment.

- **Add a Class Message:** Use this room to pose questions or to reply broadly.

Assignment Details

To open the Assignment Details page, students should build the habit of pressing Open or click the assignment title. Students would have additional details on this tab.

- Title, explanation, and deadline of an assignment.

- Students can see any file attachments or models that the instructor has produced or added for the students under your work. Note: If the instructor has created a template for use by students, students must not add or create their own except as instructed by the teacher.

- **Add:** learners can insert documents or links themselves here.

- **Create:** Learners can build new Documents, slides, Sketches, or Sheets here.

- **Turn In**: After the task has been done, students press the Turn in button and turn in.

- Insert a confidential remark, which teacher can only view

Turning In Assignments

If the instructor has allocated their version of a Google file format (Docs, Slides, Sheets, or Drawings) to a student as part of the assignment, the Google file next to the Share button will also have a Turn In option (top-right).

Note: Turn In option changes the student's ownership of the file back to the instructor, and the learner cannot edit the file again.

Learners must submit their tasks using the "Turn In" button, not by sharing with the teacher. The teacher already has access to view and edit the file. A pop-up will lead them to verify their submission when a student clicks the Turn In button.

If the teacher has assigned a Google collaborative file (the student can edit the file) or other external assignment types, instead of Turn-In, the learner will see a "Mark as Done" option. This option appears only in Google Classroom, not within the document itself.

Upon completion of the assignment, students simply click on the "Mark as Done" tab to let the teacher know that they have finished.

Note: When work is turned in or marked as done, the instructor does not get an alert or e-mail notice. If a student submits his/her work late, it is advisable to leave a personal note to inform the instructor of late work or particular circumstances.

Announcements & Questions

Announcements will show up in the Stream and are typically read-only, but if the teacher has enabled this, learners have the choice of leaving a class comment. The teacher and other students in the class are eligible for post-class feedback. If there are attachments to the post, the students may also access the folders, connections, or images. When the students are given a topic query, it should appear in the Stream automatically. In the Stream, students can see the choices below.

- Current status (not finished or finished).

- Deadline (Students can even see if the assignment is late).

- Name and Task Description.

- **Your reply:** This is where learners type in their answers. Learners must first send their answers before they can access the responses from other learners.

- **Insert a Class Message:** Use this room to pose questions or to reply broadly. You don't put in your response to the query here.

Google Calendar

Google Calendar is built within Google Classroom, making it easier for students to display work due dates in one place and more. Any task or discussion query with a due date would be automatically added to the Google Calendar for that class.

- Go to Google Classroom Menu at the top-left of your computer (three lines).

- Choose Calendar.

You can see a weekly schedule of all your lessons together here, or you can search for each lesson. You can also press on a task to go straight to the details page of that assignment.

Google Drive Folders

In Google Drive, Classroom can automatically build folders for students. You will find a master folder titled, "Classroom," within your Google.

- Inside the master-folder is a sub-folder for each class that you have joined.

- You can often notice several separate files and data within each classroom file based on what the instructor attached to the tasks.

Chapter 4: Chapter 4 Advanced Tips and Tricks to Get the Most Out of Google Classroom for Students

 I wanted to go over Google Docs before the other office productivity apps because it's the one that is probably used by most people. Google Docs is Google's word processor application (similar to the popular Microsoft Word program). Once we start diving into how Docs works, you will see that it has many of the same functionality of Word (if you are a current Word user).

How to Create a Google Doc

To access Google Docs, all you need to do is go to the Google Docs website or search for Google Docs and get to it; then, it will take you to the Docs interface. If you are not logged in, you will be prompted to enter your Gmail address and password.

Since I have logged into Docs before, it shows me my recent documents on the bottom of the screen and an option to start a new blank document or a document from one of the built-in templates. There are many templates to choose from, from resumes to letters to brochures, and so on.

Tip

Templates are a great way to see what kind of things you can do in Google Docs. Try opening one up and playing around with it to see if you can figure out how to put it together. To start using Docs, we will either need to open a recent document, create a new blank document, or create a document from one of the templates. For my example, I will use a template called Lesson Plan from the template gallery. Once I click on that template, it will open up in Docs and be ready for us to start editing.

Now you can see the toolbars and menu items that you can use when working on your documents. The options are not as extensive as the ones with Word, but there are plenty of tools to help you get the job done.

Many of the tool icons are apparent, such as the ones for changing the font type, size, and color. Plus, there are buttons to do things like center and justify the text or insert images and hyperlinks. Plus, if you need to know what a button does, hold your mouse over the button. The tooltip will appear; telling you what that button does and also give you the keyboard shortcut for that function. For example, you can see that the button allows you to insert a link in your document, and you can also press Ctrl+K on your keyboard to do the same thing.

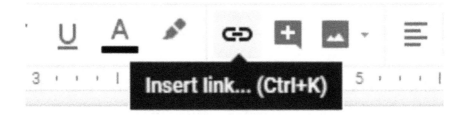

You will also notice next to the name of the document that there is an option to mark it with a star, which will mark it as starred in your Google Drive, and also allow you to access this particular document faster in the future.

Next to the star is a folder icon, which will allow you to move your document to a different folder within your Google Drive to help you keep things more organized. It is one reason you should set up your Drive before getting into the other Google apps too, so that things will make a little more sense.

At the upper right of the screen, you will see a message looking icon. This is where you can view or add any comments about this particular document. The icon to the right can be used to view your account settings or sign out of your account if needed.

On the right-hand side of the screen, there will also be some icons that are used for quick access to your calendar, Google Keep, and your Tasks. If you use these apps, this can come in handy. Otherwise, you can ignore them.

Another thing I want to mention on the right side of the screen is the Editing Mode dropdown selection.

There are three different modes to choose from:

- **Editing**: This mode is what you will be using most of the time. This mode allows you to edit your document, meaning you can add text and images, change formatting, and so on.

- **Suggesting**: If you are sharing your document with others for collaboration purposes, the Suggesting mode can make changes marked as suggested changes. Anyone with edit permissions on the document can accept or reject your suggestions. It's similar to the Track Changes feature in Microsoft Word. Todd Simms added the words of this course, which is marked with brackets above and below the text, and changes the text to read. Now there is an option to accept or reject the changes with the checkmark or the X.

- **Viewing**: This mode is used to put the document in a read-only mode where no changes can be made.

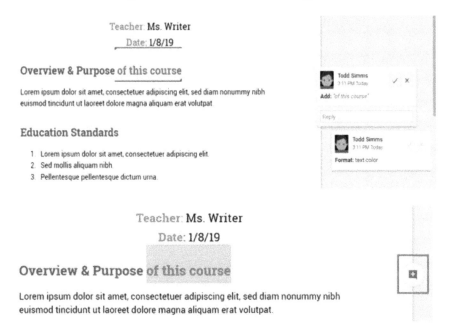

- Clicking on an object or highlighting some text will bring up an insert comment button.

- Clicking on that button will allow you to type in a comment for the particular item you selected, whether it be text or an image etc.

- After you type in your comment, it will show the right-hand side of the page, and you will have some things you or others can do with that comment.

- Clicking on Resolve will mark the comment as resolved and hide the discussion.

- Clicking on Edit or Delete are apparent, but when you click on Link to this comment, you will have with a link that you can copy and paste into an e-mail to send off to someone else so they can look over your comment. For that person to see your comment, they will need to have permission to access the document. Otherwise, they can request permission from the page the link brings them to.

Menu Items

Now I would like to go over the tools and functions that you can use from the menu items within Docs. Many of these are apparent, so I will go into more detail about the ones that might not be too obvious. Keep in mind that many of the items you will find under the various menus will be the same as what is available in the toolbars.

File Menu

The File menu is where you will find many of your administrative functions, such as opening a current document or creating a new one.

I will now briefly go over all of the items within the File menu:

- **Share**: All you need to do is type in their e-mail address and choose if they can edit, comment, view your document, and click on Send.

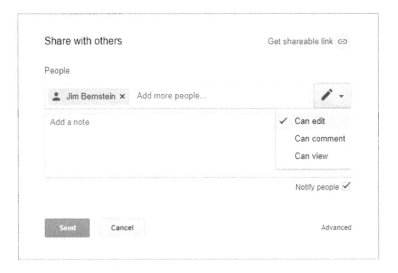

- **New**: This option brings you back where you can choose to create a new blank document or create a new document from one of the included templates.

- **Open**: This option will let you open and saved documents from your Google Drive, as well as documents that have been shared with you by others. If you want to upload a new document to work on, you can do that from here.

- **Make a copy**: This option will make a copy of the existing document in the location of your choosing. You can name the copy anything you wish. Otherwise, it will be named Copy of Document Name, there will also be a checkbox options to share the copy with the same people as the original was shared with, and also an option to copy comments and suggestions.

- **Download as**: If you want to download a copy of the document to your local computer or another device, then you can do so using this option. You have several choices as to what type of document you want to save it, such as a Word document, PDF, text file, and so on.

- **E-mail as an attachment**: If you want to send your actual document to someone rather than inviting them to view it from your account, you can use the e-mail as an attachment option.

Here you can choose what type of file you can have your attachment sent as by clicking on the down arrow under Attach as, or you can use the Paste the item itself into the e-mail option if you want the document to be displayed in the body of the e-mail.

- **Version History**: As Google Docs saves your changes, it will keep various versions of the file you want to revert to a different version, and maybe recover some changes. Clicking on the three vertical dots next to a version will allow you to copy that version or give it a specific name. You also have the option to have Docs only show named versions, so your version history only shows the versions you want to see.

- **Rename**: This option renames your document to a name of your choosing. I clicked on Rename. It highlighted the Lesson plan, allowing me to change it to something else if desired.

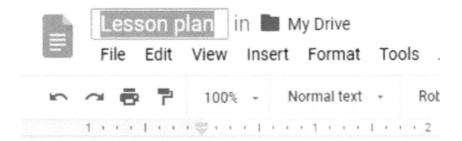

- **Move to**: Using this option does the same thing as clicking the folder icon next to the star. It will allow you to move the file to a different location on your Google Drive or move it to your local computer.

- **Move to trash**: If you want to delete your document, you can use this option. (You can recover it from your trash if you change your mind later).

- **Publish to the web**: If you would like to share your document as a read-only webpage version of the file, then this is where Publish to the web can come in handy. When you use this option, Docs will create a link when you click on Publish that you can copy and then send it to other people so they can view your document within their web browser.

Chapter 5: More Tips for Teachers and Students

Tips for Teachers

Tip 1: Learn all the ways to give feedback

Your students are going to thrive with as much feedback as you can provide them, and the classroom offers you many options for this. You can leave comments on assignments that students hand in, on the file that is submitted, through e-mail, and so much more. Consider the best places to leave feedback and let your students know so they can be on the lookout for ways to improve.

Some of the ways that you can utilize comments include:

- **Class comments**: You can do this by starting a common for the whole class on the outside of the assignment or in the announcement. It is going to be a comment that the entire course is going to see, so don't use it if you just want to talk to the individual student. It is an excellent option to use if you're going to answer a question that many people have.

- **Private comments**: you can do this by going into the file of an individual student. You will see the submissions this student has made and can click on the comment bar near the bottom. When you add a comment, the student will be the only one who can see it.

- **Comments to media**: You can do this by clicking on the file that the student submitted to you. Highlight the area and then comment on that particular part of the project. It can help you show an example of the student or explain your thoughts and how something needs to be changed.

Tip 2: Use the description feature

When creating an assignment, make sure to add a nice long description. It is where you explain what the task is all about, how to complete it, and even when the assignment is due. Often students are juggling many classes all at once, and by the time they get to the task, they have forgotten all the instructions you gave them in class, or if a student missed class that day, the description can help them understand what they missed. A good report can help to limit e-mails with questions. It can help students get started on the assignment without confusion.

Tip 3: Reuse some of your old posts

At times, you may have an assignment, question, or announcement that is similar to something you have posted before. For example, if you have a weekly reading or assess task that is pretty much the same every week, you will use the reuse option in the classroom. To do this, just click on the "+" button that is on the bottom right of the screen, and then you will then be able to select "Reuse post." Pick from a list of options that you already used for the class. If there are any modifications, such as a different due date, you can make those before posting again. When reusing the post, you have the option to create new copies of the attachments that were used in the original posting.

Tip 4: Share your links and resources

There may be times that you find a fascinating document, video, or other media that you would like your students to see, or they may need resources for an upcoming project. You want to make it easier for them to find. In this case, you should use the announcement feature. It allows all the essential documents to be listed right at the top of the classroom rather than potentially getting lost further down in assignments.

It is a great tip to use for items of interest that you would like to share with your students or for documents and files that they will need right away. If you have a resource that the students will need throughout the year, you should place it into the "About" tab to prevent it from getting lost as the year goes on.

Tip 5: Use Flubaroo

Grading can take up a lot of your time, especially when dealing with many students and multiple classes. You want to provide your students with accurate feedback as quickly as possible, but traditional teaching can make this impossible. Add-ons like Flubaroo can make this easier. When creating a quiz or test, you can use Flubaroo so that when a student submits their answers, the app will check them and provide a score right away. The student can see how well they did on the quiz and where they may need to make some changes.

This kind of add-on is best for things such as multiple choice assignments and tests. It allows the student to see what they understand right away without waiting for the teacher to correct everything. You can go back and change the grade on a particular assignment if the add-on grades incorrectly, you want to add bonus points, or for some other reason.

If you are creating assignments like discussion posts, opinions, projects, and essays, Flubaroo is not the best option for you. This app is not going to understand how to grade these projects. Since each one is more creative and doesn't necessarily have a right or wrong answer, the teacher needs to go in and grade. There are many places where you can provide feedback, even at various points of the project, to help the student make changes before the final grade.

Tips for Students

Tip 1: Pick One E-mail for all of Your Classes

Consider having a dedicated e-mail that is for all of your classes. You don't need to separate it and have an e-mail for each of your categories, but create a new e-mail that will only accept information from all classes using Google Classroom. Whenever a teacher announces they use this platform, you will use this e-mail. It helps you to keep all of your courses in one place and can prevent you from missing out on your announcements and assignments because they got lost in all your e-mails.

Tip 2: Check Your Classes Daily

As the year goes on, your teacher will probably get into a routine when they make posts, and you can check the class at that time. But it is still a good idea to stay on top of a class and check it each day. You never know when you may forget about an assignment that is almost due or when the teacher will add a special announcement for the whole class. If you only check your levels on occasion, you could miss out on a lot of valuable information along the way. Check-in daily to stay up to date and to get everything in on time.

Tip 3: Look at the Calendar

One of the first places you should go when opening up to a class on the calendar. It is going to list everything necessary that is coming your way in the few months (updated as the teacher adds new announcements and assignments) so you can plan out your time. For some students, it is easier to get a grasp on the work when it is in tablet form rather than just looking at a date in the announcements. Use this as a planning tool and check it often to see if there is anything new to add to your schedule.

Tip 4: Ask Questions for Clarification

The classroom makes it easier for students to ask the questions they need before starting an assignment. In some classes, it can be hard to find time to ask a question. When twenty or more students are asking questions at the same time, or the teacher runs out of time and barely gets the assignment out before the bell, many students may leave the classroom without any clue how to begin on a task.

With the classroom, the students can ask any questions they have when it is convenient. If they have a question about an assignment or some feedback left for a test or essay, they can comment on the task or send an e-mail or can ask it right on the assignment. The classroom has opened up many options for talking to your teacher and getting your questions answered, so don't be shy and sit in the dark when you need clarification.

Tip 5: Learn About all the Features of Google

Google has many great features that both students and teachers can take advantage of. Many people don't realize all of the different apps that are available on Google, and since these apps can be used together with the classroom and are free, it is essential to take advantage of as many as possible. Some of the best Google products that can help with learning include:

- **Gmail:** Gmail makes it easier for students and teachers to communicate about the class without sharing the information with other students.

- **Calendar:** students will be able to see at a glance when essential assignments, tests, and additional information occur in their class.

- **Drive:** This is a great place to put all tasks, questions, and other documents needed to keep up in class. Teachers can place learning materials and assignments inside for the student to see. Students can submit their jobs all in one place.

- **YouTube:** Students are used to spending time on YouTube, and teachers can use this to their advantage to find educational videos for their class. Students can either look at links that the teacher provides or search for their videos.

- **Docs:** This program works similarly to Microsoft Word, but since it is free, it can be helpful for those students who don't already have Word at home. Students can write, edit, and make changes just like on regular documents and then submit them back to the teacher.

- **Google Earth/Maps**: Explores the world around us with these two great features. Google Earth lets students learn more about the world by allowing them to look up different areas and see them from an actual satellite. Google Maps can help with Geography worldwide, or students can even create their Maps with this program.

These are just a few of the different apps available with Google that can make a difference in how students learn. While not all of them will apply to every class, a good understanding of each can help the teacher pick the right one for their quality and help them learn as much as possible.

Chapter 6: How to Set Due Dates, Manage Homework and Assignments

Creating an Assignment

1. Please log in.

2. Click on the Class.

3. Turn over the bottom Add, tap Create assignment.

4. Enter the heading and instructions.

Change the Time or Due Date of Assignment

The assignment submission due date by default is one day/next day. Changing it:

1. Click the Down arrow next to the Due Tomorrow.

2. Tap on the date, then choose the date.

3. (Optional) Press Time and choose a date to set the due period.

4. Select Due date to build a task with no due date press Delete next to a deadline.

To Assignment Attaching Materials

You can attach examples to the assignments, like Google Drive data, videos of YouTube, or links.

1. Click Attach for uploading a file, select a file and then click Upload.

2. To add an object to the Drive, like a form or document:

    a. Click the drive.

    b. Choose the object and press Add.

3. For deciding how the students link with an attachment, tap the Down arrow, select the option next to the attachment:

    a. Students can access the file: they can read the file, but they cannot modify it.

    b. File editing by students: students, also can make file changes.

    c. Create copy for every student: Students get a file copy they will modify.

4. Select YouTube to add a YouTube file, and an option is selected:

To look for the attached video

    a. Click Search for a Video.

    b. In the bar, enter keywords for searching.

c. Click Video and then press Add.

d. Add a link to the video.

e. Click for URL.

f. Type the URL in and press Add.

g. Select Link, insert the URL, press Add to append a link.

h. Press Remove next to some attachment to remove an object.

Multiple Classes Assignment Posting

1. (Optional) Press the down arrow next to the name of the class at the bottom.

2. Check the appropriate box present beside the class wanted by you to include.

How a Google Classroom Assignment is Created on Android Devices

1. Tap the Classroom.

2. Press Add Assignment.

3. Enter the heading and any guidelines.

Change the Time or Due Date of Assignment

The assignment submission date by default is one day/next day, but it can be changed.

1. Press Due date, chose another date, and touch 'Done.'

2. (Optional) touch Time choose the time and touch 'Done.'

3. Attaching materials to the assignment.

You May Attach Your Assignment to Drive Folders, Links, Photographs, or Videos of YouTube

1. Click Attach, the file is selected, and press Upload to upload a file.

2. Tap Drive, the item is tapped and Select to attach a Drive item.

3. To determine how the students communicate with the object, press view, and select an alternative next to the attachment:

    • **Students can modify files:** Students can make file changes.

- **Students can access the file**: the students can read the file, but they do not modify it.

- **For every student, create a copy:** Students get a copy of the file they will modify.

- Delete the attachment.

4. Tap Link, the URL is entered, and press Add for attaching a link.

5. Tap Upload for adding a photo.

6. Tap Camera, select or take the photo for attaching a photo and click OK.

7. Tap YouTube to add a YouTube clip, and an option is selected:

To Check for the Video Attaching

1. Tap Search for the Video.

2. In the bar, enter keywords for searching.

3. Tap Video, then tap Add.

For Attaching a Link to the Video

1. Tap on URL.

2. Enter URL, and then tap Add.

3. Next to the name of the attachment, tap view to delete an attachment, and then select Delete.

Multiple Classes Assignment Posting

1. Tap Add. beside the name of the class.

2. Select the additional Classes.

How to Build an Assignment on iOS/iPhone/iPad via Google Classroom

1. Tap the Classroom.

2. Press Add Assignment.

3. Enter the heading and any guidelines.

Change the Time or Due Date of Assignment

The assignment submission date is for one day/ next day by default, but you can change it.

1. Press Due date, pick a specific date, then tap OK.

2. (Optional) Tap Attach time, select time, then tap OK.

3. (Optional) Tap Remove Tomorrow to create some assignments without any due date.

To an Assignment Adding Materials

You can add to your assignment Drive files, links, pictures, or photos.

1. Press Attach.

2. Press Drive, then select the object to add a Drive element.

3. To determine how the students communicate with an object, tap view, select an option next to the attachment:

   • **Students can make file changes:** Students can edit files.

   • **The students can view the file**: the students can read the file, but they do not modify it.

   • **Create a copy for every student**: Students get a copy of the file they will modify.

   • Delete the attachment

4. Tap Link, the URL is entered, and press Add to attach a link.

5. Tap Select picture for adding a picture, then choose the picture. Or press the Camera and then take a picture.

6. Press Delete beside the attachment.

Schedule Assignment

If there were any reservations as to whether the Google Classroom team listens to requests from teachers, a new feature update confirms that they do! Teachers are already pushing so hard for Google Classroom schedule assignments.

Make Post

In Google Classroom, create an assignment, announcement, or a question. To add the post, click the plus icon at the bottom left of the Google Classroom.

Arrow

- Create the post and then locate the arrow next to Assign.

- Google Classroom Schedule Assignment

- Clicking the arrow gives the Schedule choice.

- Select the middle option from the menu, drop-down.

Schedule

1. Change the time and date to let them know when you want the assignment to post to the Stream. Editable is the time so you can

schedule it for the exact time you want it to
post

Multiple Classes

If the assignment is chosen to post to the multiple
classes, it'll post to all the classes. If to each class at
different times you want to have the assignment post,
you must reuse the post. Unchecking should be
remembered. Create new copies of every attachment's
checkbox. The best thing about Google Docs is that only
one version is there, and it's always current. A mess is
made of your Google Drive by creating copies.

Assignments Managing

1. Individual classes are affected by Edits.

2. Make edits in every class for multiclass
   assignments.

Note: When you update the name of an assignment, the
name of the Drive folder of the assignment won't
update, so Visit Drive to have the folder renamed.

Posted Assignment Edit

1. On the page of Classwork, click on more Edit the
   assignment

2. Enter the changes and press Save.

Scheduled Task Edit

1. On the page of Classwork, click on more Edit the assignment.

2. Enter your modifications and press Schedule.

Change Roster Distribution

1. On the page of Classwork, click on more Edit the assignment.

2. Select the assignment and type your modifications.

Changes are then saved automatically

1. Select the option:

   • Assign it right away.

   • Plan the publishing at a specified time and date (details above).

   • To retain a draft and go back to the Classwork tab, press Close at the top.

Chapter 7: Google Drive Hacks for Gmail

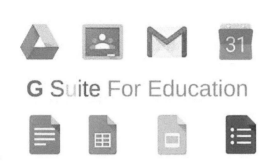

It may be easy to understand how to navigate through Google Drive functions. Still, only a few people know how to optimize them. Some people would spend hours trying to do a task that could take only seconds or minutes.

For better time management and efficiency for teachers, this covers explanatory tips to help you work better with Google Drive functions.

Here are some hacks for Gmail users.

You can Upload and Save Files and Folders

Most people know that files can be uploaded on Google Drive but may not know that you can upload folders also. To be clear, you can upload anything to Google Drive as long as you still have enough storage space.

To upload files and folders:

Open Google Drive and click on the '+ new' icon at the top-left corner. It will display the options, and then you can click on file upload. If you're working with a computer, it may be easier for you to drag the file and drop in the right pane. Files are not limited to just Word or Docs; they could also include mp3, GIFs, and other files.

You could also save yourself time and upload entire folders.

Your folder could contain several different files like a collection of video files, images, PDF documents, design files, and others.

You can Create Varying Degrees of Content

Another barely explored Google Drive function is content creation. While you can safely store your files and folders, you can create documents and other content with Google Drive. Did we say easily?

There is various contents that can be created with Drive aside from the popularly known Docs (Word Processing), Spreadsheets, and Presentation Slides.

For teachers, Google Drive provides multiple contents software to make your work more effective and more comfortable. You can do it with ease and with just a single click.

So, how do you get started? Read on to find out.

Go to the top-left corner of your Google Drive and click on the '+ New' option. You'll see the customer Docs, Sheets, and Slides options. If you want to create one of them, click on it. However, if you want to explore other options, click on More.

Here's a list of some other fantastic tools that are available on Google Drive to make all of our work easier.

- **Google Forms:** This is an essential tool for creating questionnaires or surveys. You could also take advantage of this one to create a multiple-choice quiz for your students and grade it in real-time.

- **Google Drawings**: This is a perfect tool for presenting your lesson in a more understandable format with the use of charts and graphs. It could also help you with reports and student progress analysis.

Other available tools are Google Maps, Google Sites, and others. You also take the option of connecting other applications to your drive. It is the best tool for virtual classroom collaboration.

- You could make use of pre-existing templates to save time.

Tired of spending time creating lessons from scratch? Try out professional templates on Google Drive. To start using Google Drive Templates, click on the '+ New' icon, and open a new document.

You will then have two options: a blank document or template. If you want a pre-made template, click on 'Open Template' and choose the one that best fits your intended project.

You can get easy design templates for letterheads, brochures, newsletters, proposals, letters, terms of use, job offer letters, reports, statements of work, and other uses.

If your template isn't present, you can also download more templates, courtesy of Google Drive.

You can Organize Your Files into Folders

Instead of wasting time looking for single files from the clutter, you can organize your work files into labeled folders. It makes your workspace more organized and easier to navigate.

On Google Drive, photos can be opened and labeled even while working with large files. For example, you could have a folder named 'in progress' and another called 'finished.'

Hence, while working on files, you can have them in the folder labeled 'in progress,' and when they are done, you move them to the 'finished' folder. Folders could also help you arrange files in categories. This way, you have a particular folder for student lessons and another for reports.

To do this, create new folders and drag the files you want into that folder.

If you move files to the wrong folder accidentally, Google Drive gives you the option of undoing it. Simply click the 'Undo' button and try again.

If you decide to change the place of a file from a folder, you could go to that folder and dig out the file, but that would take time. Some shortcuts could help you do this quickly and in no time. Read on to find out the Google Drive shortcuts.

You Can Use Shortcuts to Navigate Easily and Quickly

More than undoing file placements, Google Drive has a lot of shortcuts that could make navigation easier and quicker. Here are a few examples:

- First things first, you move a file to the wrong folder and can't click the Undo button. You can easily click on command + Z to cancel that move. That was easy, wasn't it?

- So you are tired of going to the '+ New' pane every time you want to create a new document? There's a quick shortcut to help you do that. Simply hit the shift key + F. This works for creating all kinds of documents.

- For search shortcuts, this is functional as you add more files to your folders. To access your search, click on the "/" button, and your search bar will immediately open.

You Could Check Your History if Something Seems Wrong

Google Drive functions allow you to access your progress history. It could be helpful when you run into issues connected to file placement or document editing. As more people gain access to your Google Drive, you may notice files and documents in the wrong folder. You might also notice updates on documents that you never did. Accessing your history could give you more information on when the change was affected and how to undo it.

To access to your history, click on the 'I' icon on the right side of your Google Drive app. Your history shows you all your recent activities within the drive, including file updates, changes, and when they took place.

You can Keep Your Drive Clean to Get More out of it

Google Drive has a storage limit. After you exhaust your storage capacity, Google will start to charge you for extra space. Keeping your drive clean can help you make more out of Google Drive without having to pay. To check how much storage you have left, check the bottom left corner of your app.

If you're not careful, your files may pile up and take all your storage space. To avoid reaching your storage limit, try cleaning up your Drive. You could schedule a monthly or weekly clean-up. Get rid of unnecessary files and files that are no longer useful. Cleaning up your Drive could also make your work a lot easier and files easier to find.

If you're running out of storage space and don't know why or what is taking up so much space, you could go to your settings and take a look at the space breakdown.

Under settings, 'General' gives you an idea of how much storage space you have used. You can view the files taking up storage space to know which to delete. If you're unable to delete any files, you could opt to upgrade storage with a paid plan.

Quick Tip: Check that website back-ups and zip files aren't taking up too much of your storage space. It would be a brilliant place to start when cleaning up your Drive.

To delete files, right-click on the file and click on remove. If you want to delete multiple files, read on for the next tip.

You Can Run an Action on Multiple Files at Once

With Google Drive, there is always an option to save time. If you realize that you want to do an action, say 'Delete,' for more than one file, you could do it all at once instead of doing it one by one. To do this, hold down the ctrl key and click on the files you want to delete.

If the files are together in succession, you could drag the mouse over them. Another choice would be to hold down the shift key, then click on the first file and the last. While the files are highlighted, right-click on them and click on 'Remove.'

After right-clicking, you will see a list of options. There is a whole lot more you can do on multiple files other than 'Delete.' Say you want to share a list of files with a colleague or your students.

What you need to do is right-click on the highlighted files and click on 'Share.' The share option could grant users access to a file or a whole folder, including all its content.

Another multiple actions you could do is move files. It is beneficial when you're organizing your Drive. You could highlight a list of files and drop them together into a new folder

There are also functions like download, make a copy or add to star.

You Could Empty Your Trash

So, while cleaning up your Drive, the 'removed' files aren't truly deleted. After files are removed, they are then stored in the 'Trash' folder. It means that the files are still taking up storage space. To permanently delete these files, don't forget to empty your trash.

You can choose to delete single files, multiple files, or the whole trash. To delete all the files in your trash, click on the 'Empty Trash' button at the top right corner.

Doing this deletes all your trashed files and creates more space on your Drive.

Chapter 8: The Best Must-Have Apps for Google Classroom

Google Classroom, online learning, and student management platform, has gradually become an accepted way of learning between teachers and students from different parts of the world.

Teachers from all over the world are now making use of the Google Classroom learning platform to create and manage their classes, as well as distribute assignments, share learning files, send feedback, and develop friendly relationships with students.

Google Classroom has made teaching tasks more comfortable, and the process of learning has become accessible to students who do not have direct access to an actual classroom.

Google has a set of cloud-based applications that have enabled teachers and students to create, collaborate, and communicate for learning. They have allowed teachers and students to be creative and enjoy the learning process. These applications enable the teacher to send information to their students with ease.

Google Classroom Applications

Several applications have been integrated with the Google Classroom learning platform, which makes it very easy to operate and access by both students and teachers alike, and it has made the sharing of information between both parties easier.

Both teachers and students have the opportunity to teach and learn from anywhere and at any time as long as they are connected to an internet-enabled device. They can always sign in to the created classroom to access the learning materials, classroom assignments, and announcements, as well as create or join in on conversations.

Thousands of education applications have, over time, been synced with Google Classroom for the benefits of teachers and students. Several apps have even launched directly with Google Classroom, which gave them visibility and a built-in audience.

Google Classroom, like other Google applications, allows integration with other third-party apps for learning. Educators can make use of these applications alongside Google Classroom to share and distribute assignments, announcements, and course materials.

There are various reasons why Educators should use Google Classroom alongside other applications to make the process of learning more accessible. Primarily, it helps make the learning process diversified and easily accessible across different platforms for the students.

It also allows you to link your favorite websites to your Google Classroom, and it makes it easier to search and retrieve information from these websites and add them to your Google Classroom.

How to Use Google Classroom with Other Applications

Not all the apps integrate with Google Classroom. There is a wide variety of educational apps that are using them with Google Classroom is usually as simple as signing in, creating your materials, and then clicking a button to share the material/post/creation/quiz in Google Classroom. Some of the apps that are integrated are free, while others work on paid subscriptions. Your school may already be using some of these applications, making it very easy for you, as the teacher, to add them to your Google Classroom.

How can you use these applications alongside Google Classroom? You can follow the steps listed below:

1. Go to Google Classroom settings to view the list of apps supported by Google. Or, navigate to the website or application you are interested in using with Google Classroom and see if it is supported.

2. Create an account on the application or website you want to link to your Google Classroom

3. After creating an account, create the activity you would want to share with your classroom, whether that is an announcement, assignment, learning resource, reference, etc.

4. Once you have created your activity, search for the share button that will link the third-party application to your Google Classroom account.

For the integration to take place, you have to grant permission for the app to link to your classroom when asked.

5. When the connection has been made between your Google Classroom and the other app, you can then go ahead and create, for example, a quiz for your students on a quiz making an application and share it on any of your classes on Google Classroom.

There is a wide variety of apps that can be integrated with Google Classroom to streamline the learning process and enhance your materials. Read about some of these fantastic apps and what they can do for you in the following list:

1. **Quizizz:** This is an Ed-tech app that enables teachers to create and assign quizzes games to their students for them to join and play. It is a way of learning that is fun for students and encourages their active participation. With Quizizz, teachers can access their students' performance through these fun assessments.

2. **Alma:** This is an educative application that was the first student information system to have been integrated with Google Classroom. With Alma, teachers can sync all assignments and grades in an organized manner for future reference and easy access.

3. **BookWidgets:** This application provides teachers with attractive educational templates. With over 40 templates, teachers

can make use of this app in their Google Classroom to engage their students in interactive lectures.

4. **Classcraft:** Classcraft is an app that is integrated with Google Classroom that helps teachers increase student participation in the learning process by importing the class from Google Classroom to Classcraft. In this app, the students become players in a game in which they are made to turn in their assignments quickly, and the grades and classroom results of each student are recorded as game points.

5. **Flipgrid:** This is an application that can be synchronized with Google Classroom. It creates a message board described as a "grid" that contains questions that are set like discussions for students to respond to through 90-second recorded videos. The video grid will then appear in the classroom. Teachers can also share links from Google Classroom to Flipgrid, and also you can add these links to assignments in your Google Classroom.

6. **Kami:** Kami has been integrated with Google Classroom and allows teachers to distribute learning/course materials, assignments, worksheets, and other resources to students in PDF format for easy assessment. It then allows students to collaborate and annotate the documents shared with them interactively.

Students can highlight pane, draw (great for math worksheets!), and even leave voice recordings or videos inside the document.

7. **Little SIS for Classroom:** Little SIS is an app that integrates with Google Classroom to help school administrators manage and view their school rosters and classrooms across all their teachers. Administrators can help organize and support their teachers in the app by archiving classes, managing teachers, viewing school rosters, and tracking classroom usage.

8. **Listenwise:** This is an app that can be synced with Google Classroom to aid learning through the sharing of audio materials like podcasts and public radio broadcasts to enhance the students' listening skills. The app is great for achieving optimum learning objectives through listening.

9. **Nearpod:** It is a great app that allows teachers to create quality learning content through videos, images, polls, and other forms of interactive presentations. It can help engage your students in Google Classroom and increases their participation.

10. **Padlet:** This is an online app that allows teachers and students to interact by sharing links, web content, pictures, etc., which can be shared with Google Classroom through the backpack version for schools. It helps foster discussions and group project collaboration.

11. **Plagiarism Check:** This app can integrate with Google Classroom for teachers to detect plagiarism in their students' assignments. It can also identify incorrect grammar, word substitution, and arrangements. It is mainly used to correct these grammar/sentence mistakes and ensure the originality of students' work.

12. **Share to Classroom Chrome Extension:** This application allows teachers and students who make use of the Chrome browser to share links, media files, and other learning resources from Chrome to Google Classroom. Teachers can easily share or pin a web page to an assignment or a lesson posted on the Classroom.

13. **PBS Learning Media**: This is a learning app that provides teachers with thousands of learning materials to enhance the learning process and improve the student learning process. You can also share these learning materials to your Google Classroom for students to access.

Other Google Classroom applications include the following:

- Peardeck

- Tynker

- Khan academy

- Quizlet

- OpenEd

- LucidPress

- NetTrekker

- Math games

- And more!

All of these and more are applications that can be integrated with Google Classroom. They are all aimed at helping teachers manage their Google Classroom effectively, engaging students, and make them more actively involved in classroom activities.

Chapter 9: Best and Must Have Extensions and Tools for Google Classroom

There are so many functions in Google Classroom that you can use, and here we will tell you about all the essential functions and applications that you can use in the classroom.

Add Materials

The best thing about Google Classroom is that you can attach various videos, pools, PDFs, and other items from a Google Drive. With this drawing, students can write notes and even highlight various elements in PDF files in the Classroom to make it easier.

Adjust Class Color

Themes and colors of classes are something you can integrate into the classroom. In this case, you can go to the setting and then choose the default color or theme for your class. It helps if you can are working with multiple classes and want to make sure that you are providing information to the correct class.

Appointment Calendar

The assignment calendar is designed to organize students and teachers better. Each time a teacher creates something in a Google class with a date, you will immediately receive it in the class calendar. It is easy to find by going to the more menu (three-lined button_ in the left corner of the screen, and selecting Calendar. After displaying, you can see all the assigned work, whether it is a teacher who assigns work for the class or a student who receives work from the teacher.

New Work Area

There are tasks in the new workspace in Google classroom that have not been completed in one place. If the teacher has not yet rated the assignment, it will be there, which is suitable for students who are curious, regardless of whether something was evaluated. In the same manner, if the students have not yet passed something, it will also be displayed there, it is useful for the teacher to find out what they need to evaluate; it is useful for students, too, who need to find out what they need to finish.

Communication with Others

Communicating with parents and students is that Google classroom does with dignity, despite the lack of animated features. Students can post messages to the audience stream, which in many cases, can be a good discussion board. It is useful if you do want your question to be answered immediately, or it is necessary. Many times, if you need to contact the teacher directly, there is a way to send him an e-mail, and teachers can do the same. Teachers also moderate the flow, and you can attach media to each of them. Gmail also allows students and teachers to communicate on the interface. I. addition, with the advent of classroom applications, this also allows for greater integration.

Course Archive

You can also archive courses with this. Using Google Classroom, at the end of a semester or year, you can select a course, go to setting, and archive if from there. It has been removed from the main home page, but not permanently deleted, so teachers can look at the current year and find any assignments that they want to save. Removing a class eliminated it, and many teachers decide not to, especially if they have assignments that they enjoyed in the previous semester.

Organizational Flow

The classroom has introduced a theme feature that allows the teacher to be better organized their workflow.

Each time an ad is created; teachers can assign a topic to each post and allow it to be organized. Whenever it is created, the theme will be to the left of the stream, and when it is selected m, the theme will be displayed. It allows teachers to better-organized content within the course so that you can organize the lesson in different units. It is great for History or Biology teachers who typically need different units or everything they go through.

Share In Class

The sharing extension of the class is available to teachers who use laptops or Chromebook in the classroom. This extension allows teachers to display screens and work in the classroom so that teachers can share the website with a computer. They can essentially click on the extensions, and from there, they decided to click on the teacher at the end. The teacher receives a notification that he will show the screen, and from there, teachers can do the same by showing the students their screen. It is no longer embarrassing to show the screen and hopes that the students will follow it. Everything happens right there.

Activity Learn

It is an application that works great with Google Classroom. It is good not only for languages, but also for English, Social Science, and even biology. You can even mosaic, take the whole class, and even carefully read sine different aspects. Teachers can use this app if they want to bring some cool and integrated classroom activities. Besides, all tasks are synchronized with Google Classroom.

Aladdin

It is more for teachers than for students, but Google Classroom is fully integrated with Aladdin. In this way, teachers can plan role books, create grades and write reports. The teacher can also quickly find information, which means that they can find out the student's enrollment date, information about their parents, class, or staff, as well as any relevant singular documents. The role book will also even be integrated with other applications. It allows you to send alerts, especially if they are in other classes, about any trends of students. It also helps encourage students' attendance so that the students feel better, and this creates an integrated learning system for students and teachers.

GoGuardian

It is a great tool not only for teachers but also for administrators and even consultants. You can filter settings for students to get fewer false-positive and even provided better class management with additional tools. When geolocation is turned on, you can recover any devices that have been lost or stolen. It is good if you want to use a laptop at school. For teachers, this also allows students to show you what they are doing in real-time, create an activity schedule, as well as some scenes that, in essence, can improve jobs and be less distraction. With GoGuardian, you can integrate this with Google Classroom to ensure that students create a better environment for themselves; as a result, teachers are also less distracted.

One-Click Worksheets

With each worksheet, you can create separate documents with one click. This is a good feature that saves you time, so you do not need to copy everything for each student, as can be annoying.

Class Resource Page

One of the good things about Google Classroom is that you can always create a class resources page for any documents you need to use with your class, including rules and the curriculum. How do you do this? You go to the page with classes, and from there you select settings, and then add class materials with a heading, which will help to organize the class a little better. You can always add several different resources under a single name and then add the different names each time. Then you can join and then select the appropriate icon. You can select the item you want to add from there and then either upload or add. To Place a link there, you can always click on it or add a link. You can click X to remove the attachment and then click the option to publish. If it is in each section, it allows students to visit it at any time, which is ideal if they need to review the curriculum again.

Grade Export

You can always export the grades you have to Google Sheets or to a CSV file to see all grades at once. You can do this only on the computer version, but not on the mobile version. To do this, you click on your class, go the classwork Assignment, and Select to view. You want to go to Work with Students and then click on the Gear icon, and from there, you want to copy all the grades to Google Sheets. You can see the spreadsheet in the folder on the disk.

If you want to export grades to a CSV file, you do the same. You can choose whether you want to download specific grades as CSV, or if you want to load all grades of tasks as CSV for them to be in the download folder. Therefore, you can import then from the outside.

Creation Individual Assignments

The Google Classroom also allows teachers to create individual assignments. In turn, this allows students to have personal assignments if they need it, which is good if there us a chance that they need to do something specific and you can use it for ads. It is quite nice. And you will realize that when you use it, it is easy to implement. It is easy to organize your assignments.

Alma

It is another student's information system, but it is the first to integrate with Google Classroom fully. During the integration process, teachers can use this to synchronize grade and assignment, and can also be used with teacher teams to manage everything in the neighborhoods and school that are nearby, which provide a better organization. This is good because it will demonstrate various trends and allow you to see what is happening, which is very good if you want to keep track of everything that happens in school.

Curiosity from Beacon Solutions

It is an application that allows students to get the necessary knowledge easily, and this is one of the best applications for Google Classroom. Curiosity is that it is ideal for those students who do not want to stop learning, and you can learn a lot by using this. There are 5000 different articles and a million different videos on any conceivable topic so that you can use them at almost all levels of education, regardless of the subject. Regardless of whether you use it for science, history, or something else, there are so many different pieces of content, amazing videos, and articles that will explain the subjects and teachings much better and more usefully.

Discovery Education

It is an application that provides digital multimedia textbooks, training materials, and videos on a very different subject. The most basic disciplines include Math and Science, are available here. It is also a great streaming resource, and it even contains modules, personalized instructions, and recommendations to help. It is not just a streaming source; it also has interactive features that help you complete tasks, including creating skills, sound clips, and even assignments and grades. It allows you to convert teaching in the classroom from a more static experience to an exciting one.

Chapter 10: Tips for Classroom Management and Instructional Forms

Google Classroom allows you to extend the blended learning experience in a variety of ways, and come in 2017; teachers can create an incredible number of ways to enhance a student's grasp of school subjects and increase learning capabilities. The possibilities are endless where Google is concerned.

Google's biggest asset is its simplicity and ease of use. Using the various Google applications doesn't require a textbook to learn it, as with Google Classroom, all other apps are simple to set up, quick to learn, and saves time and energy to get things done and organize your various files and documents. We will share ten best practices for Google Classroom that you can employ to fully make use and take advantage of this pioneering online education tool.

Reduce the Carbon Footprints of Your Class

The idea of Google Classroom is to make things easier for teachers and students alike when learning things. It takes the conventional classroom and places it on the online sphere and enables students and educators to create spreadsheets and presentations, online documents, and it makes sharing and communicating easier. Creating and sharing things eliminates the need for printing. Schools use a lot of papers, but utilizing Classroom enables you to remove the necessity of paper for simple things. Have an assignment? Save some trees, time, and money by creating them in the Classroom, distributing it to your students in your Classroom.

Distribute and Collect Student's Homework Easily

The whole point of creating the assignments via Google Classroom is so that you can distribute it and collect the assignments quickly. Yes, you can say that you could get it done via e-mail too. But Classroom enables all these things to be done in one place. You'll know who has sent an assignment, who have passed their deadline, and who needs more help with their work. It's all about lessening the hassle in your life.

Utilizing the Feedback Function

With instant access, teachers can clarify doubts, concerns, and misconceptions their students may have by providing feedback as and when students need it. As teachers, you eliminate possible issues that might arise while students are doing their assignments. It reduces the headache you might have upon receiving the assignments that don't meet the requirements. Assignments that are handed in that have issues can be immediately rectified as well, through private one-on-one feedback with the relevant student.

Create Your Personalized Learning Environment

The main benefit of Google Classroom is the freedom that it gives teachers. Very often, teachers are required to follow the national syllabus forwarded by the Department or Ministry of Education in a country. While this is rightly done for the sake of uniformity and to ensure students across the country have access to the same level of education, utilizing Classroom, on the other hand, gives teachers the freedom to add and create a different environment for learning.

Teachers can focus on using different materials, subjects and cater to the different levels and needs of students. If you are using Google Classroom, then make sure you use this aspect to your fullest advantage. You would be able to endorse a personalized learning system by giving your students different learning preferences such as choices of submitting answers, various types of online assignments, and using online resources.

Encourage Real-World Applications

Encourage students to submit their assignments using real-world material, whether it's a series of videos or photos, a compilation of multimedia applications. Using the many different apps out there to create amazing online presentations are just some of the things that students can do that will increase their learning tendencies and spark online discussions within the Classroom. It enables the students to apply and implement assignments that they have done in their real lives.

Allow Shy Students to Participate

As teachers, we know which students are more extroverted than the other. Sometimes in conventional classroom settings, the shy kid or the kid with self-esteem issues or those that lack confidence has problems participating in classroom activities, speaking out, or even raising their hand to answer questions. Google Classroom gives a safety barrier for students that fall into this category but allowing them to be more open with discussing and expressing themselves. As the teacher, you can also find creative ways to encourage these students to open up via game-based learning to promote trust, openness, teamwork, and collaboration.

Allow Coaching

Some students need more coaching and a little bit more explanation. If you know some students in your class that needs it, you can give them different instructions by privately messaging them. You can always follow up with them while they are doing their assignments just to check if they are on the right track. Additionally, you can also invite another teacher to collaborate and help with coaching your students.

Interactive Activities Using Google Classroom

The more and more you use Google Classrooms, the more you will be able to use Classrooms in many more ways than just connecting with your students and creating assignments.

Google Classroom, combined with other Google products such as Google Slides, can deliver powerful interactive user experiences and deliver engaging and valuable content.

Teachers looking to create engaging experiences in Google Classroom can use Google Slides and other tools in the Google suite of products to create unique experiences.

Here are some exciting ways that you can use Google Classroom and Google Slides to create an engaging learning experience for your students.

Create eBooks via PDF

PDF files are so versatile, and you can open them in any kind of device. Want to distribute information only for read-only purposes? Create a PDF! You can use Google Docs or even Google Slides for this purpose and then save it as a PDF document before sending it out to your classroom.

Create a Slide Deck Book

Make your textbooks paperless, too, not just assignments. Teachers can derive engaging and interactive content from the web and include it in the slide deck books, upload it to the Google Classroom, and allow your students to access them. Make sure to keep it as read-only.

Play Jeopardy

This method has been used in plenty of Google Classroom. Eric Curts created the idea, a Google Certified Innovator, created this template that you can copy into your own Google Drive to customize with your questions and answers. You can keep scores on another slide that only you can control.

Create Game-Show Style Games

Another creative teacher came up with a Google Slide of 'Who Wants to Be a Millionaire?' The template allows you to add in your questions and get students to enter the answers in the text box. Again, you keep the score!

Use Animation

Did you know you can create animations in your Google Slide and share it in one Classroom? This tutorial shows you how. You can also encourage your students to create an animation to explain their assignments. It is making them push boundaries and think out of the box.

Create Stories Sand Adventures

Using Google Slides and uploading them to Google Classroom to tell a story. Turn a question into a story and teach your students to create an adventure to describe their decision for the outcome of the character in their story. The stories can be a certain path that the students have chosen for the character of a story that explains the process of finding a solution.

Using Flash Cards

Flashcards are great ways to increase the ability to understand a subject or topic. Do you want to create an interactive session on Google Classroom using flashcards? You can start by utilizing Google Sheets, which gives you a graphic display of words and questions and then to reveal the answers, all you need to do is click. Compared to paper flashcards, these digital flashcards allow you to easily change the questions, colors as well as the answers of the cards depending on what you are teaching the class. Digital flashcards also are an interactive presentation method that is guaranteed to engage your Classroom and bring about a new way of teaching using Google Classroom's digital space.

Make vocabulary lessons, geography lessons, and even history lessons fun and entertaining with digital flashcards.

Host an Online Viewing Party

Get your students to connect to the Classroom at a pre-determined date and time when there is a noteworthy performance, play, or even movie that is related to the subjects you are teaching in your class. Let them view the video together and also interact with them by adding questions to your Google Classroom and allowing your students to reply to you in real-time. This way, you can see assess them on their reflections, level of understanding, and their observations. You can also give your interpretation of the scene and explain it again to students who do not quite understand.

There is no limit to what a teacher can do with Google Classroom and the entire Google suite of apps, whether its Google Slides or Google Calendar or even Google Maps. The only thing you would need is creativity and the desire to give your student a different experience when using Google Classroom.

Chapter 11: Google Classroom vs. Apple Classroom

Finally, let's talk about Google Classroom versus Apple Classroom. Google Classroom is the focus of this book, but how does it stack up to Apple Classroom? Well, read on to find out.

The Hardware Difference

The most significant difference that you'll run into is the hardware elements. Apple Classroom is free for iPad, and the classroom involves using multiple different iPad. The teachers will put these on the device, allowing students to use them as an integrative tool. The teacher iPad is a collection of these powers to give a learning experience. Mostly, it's similar to Google Classroom, and once it is arranged, it's connected to devices, and the iPad is shared. Then, once the session is done, it can be signed out. It's a way to keep students focused, shows students different screens, and it can share documents with the class through the use of AirDrop. It shows student work on Apple TV, resets the passwords for students, creates groups of students based on the apps they use, and allows teachers to create groups and teams. It's a way to have Apple within the classroom. Through the use of the IPAD, it's more collaborative directly within the direct learning atmosphere.

Suitable for Lower Level Grades

Now you'll notice immediately that the only similarity is that they both include the word "classroom." It means that Apple Classroom is more of a direct classroom tool, and it helps teachers show apps and pages to students who might have trouble with them, and shows off the work that's there. Teachers in upper grades benefit from this because it monitors the activity. Still, the thing is students can find out if the teacher is watching very quickly. It's more of a direct device to use for learning within the classroom. In contrast, with Google Classroom, it focuses on both in and outside the classroom.

Google Classroom Focuses on Organization

One big part of Google Classroom is the organization element. It is all collaborated with Google drive, which means that learning is based on connections and education is based on the organization rather than directly in a physical classroom. Google Classroom makes it easy for teachers to assign the work and allows students to have better organization for assignments. It also allows them to get updates faster. You get the opportunity to go paperless too, which is a big plus. Google Classroom focuses on showing work that needs to be done, any grades they have, and any assignments that they missed. It's more of a tool for better organization of the student body over everything else.

Apple Classroom has More Interactive Lessons

For those teachers who want to have a more engaging class, that's where Apple Classroom may work better. For example, if you're teaching a younger crowd, it may be better to have Apple Classroom, because let's face it, do first graders need to navigate Google drive and submit documents? Course not. They would benefit more from Apple Classroom since it involves showing the App and allows teachers to teach. Students focus on what the teacher is teaching. It's focused as well on interacting with the student. It shows the assignment that they work on, giving teachers a chance to look at each of the pieces of work that the student does and the most recently used options. There even the screen view that shows the iPad: and it is an excellent way to keep the direct focus of the students within the classroom.

So if you're a more interactive-lesson focused teacher, such as you're teaching students the shades, or want students to not screw around in class, the Apple Classroom device may be a better option for you. If you're a teacher who is more interested in having essays, homework, and other elements easily organized in one place, then yes, Google Classroom may be more your style.

Google Classroom Allows for Multiple Devices to Be Used

It is possible to get tablets for Google Classroom, but if you want to have students work on something right away, they totally can. The beauty of Google Classroom is that it's not attached to a brand. You can get Google on your computers, and installing chrome is super easy. With that, you are given way more options on using it. Google Classroom can be downloaded as an app too on your device, meaning that if you've got a phone, tablet, or whatever, you're necessarily free to use it with whatever you want. That's what's so lovely about it, because students can work on assignments right away, and from there, submit it to the teacher. It is much more interactive and is perfect for a classroom with multiple smart devices.

The problem with Apple is that it's a brand. You are mainly working only with the Apple brand, meaning that it's highly limited. After all, not everyone may have a Mac or an IPAD, so it doesn't have as much use as, say, Google Classroom does.

You Don't Have to Choose

The reality of this, though, is that there are some key differences. You can choose based on needs, with Apple classroom being more of a focus directly within the class environment itself, and Google classroom being more on workflow and assignments. They're two different tools, but comparing it is like comparing apples with oranges, which is a bit different from your average device comparison since they are often pitted against each other in the technology realm. The truth is you shouldn't have to choose between them because some teachers benefit from both. The answer is you shouldn't choose one or the other. If you want to get both or, if the district can handle both, get them. But, if you're a teacher for a younger group of students, Apple Classroom works. If you're a teacher for older students, Google Classroom works.

Apple Classroom and Google Classroom are two very different types of software. Still, both of them accomplish the goal of helping children learn better, so they can use these skills to better their lives now and in their future learning attempt and studies that they will embark on.

FAQs About Google Classroom

While using the Google Classroom, before I can see deadlines for each assignment, I have to open each subject before the due date can be visible. Is it possible to view all of the deadlines from the homepage without having to undertake the long process of viewing each assignment one by one?

Answer: You can access all of the due assignments at once. In other to be able to view all of the new assignments for all of your classes and the dates in which they will be due, click on the 'Menu' button (represented by three horizontal lines) located at the top left corner of your Google Classroom homepage. Go ahead to select the 'To-Do' option, and it automatically reveals all of the due assignments and classes at once. Select the 'All Classes' option located at the top, helps you to filter a couple of particular classes in your classroom.

Is it possible to have works you have done moved or archived into your topic folders?

Answer: Your most recent topics can be moved to the top for your students to be able to access easily if only you are making use of Topics in the tab 'Classwork.' Topics and assignments cannot be archived; however, you can decide to have a new topic created and have it

110

named 'Archive.' You can select any assignment that to move it to the folder 'Archive'. You can then replace the topic it is in with Archive. Archived topics cannot be organized into folders as it still will not be made accessible to the students; hence they are at a disadvantage when this is done. Topics should rather be reordered rather than doing that. There are various ways of having your topics ordered and organized either by Units or Weekly.

As a regular company and not a school, can Google Classroom be used as a tool for classes that are paid for? Is that okay and possible?

Answer: This is okay and possible. A good number of people always use Google Classroom as a tool to make others have access to contents and services which they provide. There is no known restriction on this as the Google Classroom is available to people who use Gmail.

How do students get to complete an assignment that has a worksheet attached to them?

Answer: It is possible to make an extra copy of the assignment for each of your students if the attached worksheet is a Google Document.

Once you make this possible, each student will have access to an individual copy, and this copy is what can be shared between the teacher and the students. Once the students are done with their assignments and ready to copy, they would select the 'Turn In' option and then see their submission. All the teacher has to do is to select the assignment.

Once students have their assignments turned in, it is observed that there are colored wedges (white, blue, grey, or red) at the bottom of the work of the students, and why does this happen?

Answer: This is not an issue. The colors just signify the types of documents that have been submitted. A document with a green wedge would signify Google Sheets. In contrast, one with a blue wedge would signify Google Doc and another with an orange wedge will signify Google Slides, and so on.

Does Google Classroom monitor each student's activity in the classroom? Activities like how long a student has been logged in the classroom or the number of people logged in at a particular time?

Answer: The Google Classroom does not have this feature added yet. It can only inform the teacher of how well a student has turned in their assignments for a given class.

For courses and contents included upon creating a Google Classroom, do I own the intellectual right to my contents or Google?

Answer: Once you have created the Google Classroom, all of your content belongs to you. Google has only provided a platform for you to interact with your students; however, you have the sole right to all of your content and can decide to remove them from the Google Classroom unto any other platform of your choice.

Can teachers make use of the Google Classroom to make live classes just like the Zoom app?

Answer: This is not possible. The Google Classroom does not support the live feature; however, teachers can only leave assignments for the students who get notified immediately and can then have access to the assignments.

Can teachers make extra copies of created assignment materials in their Google Classroom?

Answer: It is possible to create extra copies of assignments when using the Google Classroom. The teacher can attach attachments, links to other resources or websites, videos on YouTube, and Google Drive files to the assignments.

As a parent or guardian, can one sign up for the Google Classroom and have access to the Google Classroom, the engagements, communications, comments, and other activities?

Answer: It is not possible to sign up for the Google Classroom as a parent or guardian. The teacher or the domain administrator will then send an invitation to your e-mail inviting you to the Google Classroom as a guardian (guardian e-mail summaries). However, this does not give you access to the classroom itself. All that the invitation does is to help you track your student's (ward's) progress in the classroom as you receive daily or weekly summaries of the activities of your ward in the class, classwork, and if they have any work missing.

Conclusion

If you are not a regular user of Google, using Google Classroom is one piece of cake. Aside from being provided via the Chrome browser, it can also be used from all laptops, cell phones, and tablets. Teachers may add as many learners as they want. They can create Google Documents to handle assignments and updates, upload YouTube videos, add links, or download files from Google Drive very easily. It will be equally simple for learners to log in and collect and turn in assignments.

Clean Interface, and User-friendly

Google Classroom invites you while remaining loyal to clean Google layout standards, in an atmosphere where even minute detail about the design is simple, intuitive, and user-friendly. It goes undoubtedly with the saying that users at Google will feel right at home.

An Excellent Device to Comment On

For a variety of online courses, the learners may comment on specific locations inside images. Teachers can also create URLs for new comments and use them for further discussion online. It has been shown that technology engages students. Google Classroom can help students get involved in the learning process and remain active. For example, if teachers have students answering questions in the Classroom, other students will comment on those answers and expand thought for both students.

It is for Everyone?

Educators can also enter Google Classroom as learners, which mean that you can set up the Google Classroom for you and your co-teachers. You may use it for faculty meetings, exchanging knowledge, or **professional development.**

Language and Competencies

When the teacher who produces the class or group of students shares content, teachers may take charge of the language levels and keep them related to their learner community, using language at all levels. Teachers can slowly develop the learning environment and distribute the course materials at their classes' speed, depending on the subject requirements and group profile. The choice of which students they are inviting to specific categories enables teachers to delegate work based on their students' particular learning needs. Teachers can build courses of up to 1000 students and 20 teachers, allowing teaching by a team where appropriate.

Content of Language Learning

A handy feature of Google classroom is that it helps students go through their work once they've submitted it. Teachers will get updates about the students' reworks or feedback on something they find difficult. It ensures they can give the students who need their attention and give them more opportunities to show their learning, operating at the right speed. Teachers can easily discern knowledge by determining which students may need extra help, who might want to work with response grids of model responses. The Google Translate plugin for the Classroom is also available to English language teachers.

Exposure to an Online World

A lot of colleges today expect students to take at least one online class during their degree research. If one gets a Master's degree in education, some of their online coursework might be eligible. Sadly, many of the students never had any online education experience. At a young age, teachers should make sure that their students have as much exposure to the online world as possible. Google Classroom is a simple way for students to assist with this change because it's super user-friendly, making it a perfect technology intro.

Differentiation

Google Classroom is an ideal resource for differentiation, as teachers can set up several different classrooms. If teachers focus on a topic in the Classroom and have groups that focus on two different levels, they can simply build two different classes. It means they can reach out to those who struggle with their kind of job without making them feel bad or dumb.

It can help teachers offer assignments on a more individual basis and reach out to some students. They can even break people into groups where teachers think they can work the best together. Google Classroom is a perfect, versatile way to make sure every student gets what they need. As instructors see fit, they can quickly delete and recreate classes.

Saves Time and Cost

Students lose out on all of the 'hidden' costs of studying at an institution by taking online courses with Google Classroom. It includes travel costs (which in some cases are very high), the costs of printing out assignments, and so on, and the stationary and notebook costs.

Although it is difficult to determine how high these costs would be before the students enroll in a course, some important considerations should be considered. More specifically, how far a student would drive to an educational institution every day (and how much parking fees if they're commuting by car). If that turns out to be a significant number, they could save money by taking online courses.

Most students find that taking Google classes saves them a lot of time since they work from home-no time is spent on regular commuting. They can even take on a part-time job if they have any spare time to earn while studying. It is perfect for those looking to maintain some kind of stable income while at the same time acquiring additional qualifications through Google Classroom.

Limitations of Google Classroom

Complex account management

Google Classroom doesn't enable multi-domain access. You can't sign in to access your personal Gmail; you need to sign in to Google Apps for Education. Consequently, if you already have your own Google ID, managing Google Accounts can be challenging. For example, if your Gmail contains a Google document or a picture and you want to share it in the Google Classroom, you need to save it separately on your device's hard drive, log out, and then log in with your Google Classroom account again. That is a trouble.

Too much 'Googlish'

Google users can get confused for the first time, as there are several buttons with icons that are only familiar to Google users.

Also, despite improved collaboration between Google and YouTube, which dramatically helps with video sharing, support for other standard tools is not built-in. You can find it annoying that you need to convert a primary Word document to a Google Doc to work with. In the Google Classroom environment, you'll only find yourself relaxed as long as the resources you're using fit with Google services.

Problems editing

When you create an assignment and send it to the learners, the learners become the document's "owners" and can edit it. It means they can erase any part of the assignment they choose, which may create problems, even if it happens unintentionally. Also, after you edit a post, students don't get a notification.

Also, there is no direct video recording option. It would be helpful to quickly and directly record voice and video messages into the Classroom at Google. Users can record the videos outside the Classroom and then upload them as an attachment.

Sharing work with learners

Learners cannot share their work with their classmates unless they become "owners" of a document, and even then, they will have to accept sharing options, which will create a rift if they want to share a report with their 50 + classmates say.

Limited integration

Google has restricted integration options and still needs to expand these options.

Updates are not automated

The event feed does not automatically update, so learners have to check and regularly refresh to avoid missing important announcements.

There are both advantages and limitations of Google Classroom. Nevertheless, benefits certainly outweigh the drawbacks. Despite safeguards in place to prevent the spread of the virus, and the school year potentially canceled for thousands of students, Google Classroom is an integrating spot, considering the current state of affairs. Its usage is safe. Educators can post in an ad-hoc fashion all the essential materials, assignments, and quizzes. The software may assist private tutors, as well as home-school parents.

Lightning Source UK Ltd.
Milton Keynes UK
UKHW052129281220
376007UK00001B/13

9 781801 546706